POSTCARD HISTORY SERIES

Lost
California

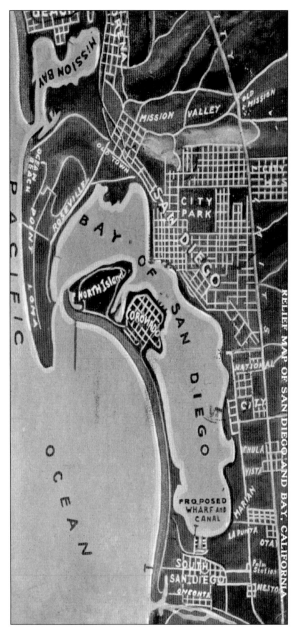

This map, which was printed in 1909, is emblematic of changes in San Diego over the last century. Aside from a lack of freeways on the map, there is a "proposed wharf and canal" in South San Diego (now Imperial Beach) that never came to fruition. City Park would be renamed through a contest in 1910 to Balboa Park. Also, the Spanish Bight that separated North Island from the rest of Coronado would be filled in during World War II. (Courtesy of the John and Jane Adams Postcard Collection, San Diego State University Special Collections & University Archives.)

ON THE FRONT COVER: This black-and-white image is of a man in an automobile on a street looking at the camera. Behind him is Stump House, a structure made from a 50-foot-long redwood tree. The Stump House was a popular restaurant and tourist attraction in Eureka, California, until it was torn down in the 1990s. (Courtesy of the John and Jane Adams Postcard Collection, San Diego State University Special Collections & University Archives.)

ON THE BACK COVER: The Hotel San Carlos, "a beautiful nine story fire-proof building of Spanish architecture, situated on the heart of Monterey" (as described on the back of the postcard), was built in 1926 and torn down in the 1980s. (Courtesy of the John and Jane Adams Postcard Collection, San Diego State University Special Collections & University Archives.)

POSTCARD HISTORY SERIES

Lost California

Erik Beck

ARCADIA
PUBLISHING

Published by Arcadia Publishing
Charleston, South Carolina

Printed in the United States of America

Library of Congress Control Number: 2023937739

For all general information contact Arcadia Publishing at:
Telephone 843-853-2070
Fax 843-853-0044
E-mail sales@arcadiapublishing.com
For customer service and orders:
Toll-Free 1-888-313-2665

Visit us on the Internet at www.arcadiapublishing.com

For Veronica and Thomas, who keep me from being lost,
and for Phil Lampi, who understands the pure joy of research

Contents

ACKNOWLEDGMENTS

Many thanks go to the Digital Collections department at San Diego State University, which gives me work and pays me to do it: Lisa Lamont, Devan McGirr, and Matt Ferrill. Work is easier when you have a great boss and a great team.

Thanks also to Katie Romabiles, who ingested a lot of these postcards in our digital repository, and Arel Lucas, who paved the way by working on the postcards before I came on board. Thanks must also go to the students who scanned many of the postcards: Cynthia Le, Miki Sanchez, Isabella Hodges, Sheetal Rani Prasad, and Lucy Breitweiser. Thanks go as well to Scott Walter and Patrick McCarthy for their support of the project.

I suppose I must thank my parents for being born in California and moving me here from New York when I was six, even though I was not happy about it at the time. My mother's interest in genealogy and my father's knowledge of history have both spurred my interest in a state where my roots go back for eight generations. It was a lot easier to move here the second time because of that.

I could not do work like this without the support of people like John Ramirez, Susannah Gavin, Erin Faulder, Phoebe Kowalewski, Anne Sauer, Krista Ferrante, Eliot Wilczek, and Ivan and Rochelle Zirdum.

This project would not exist without the John and Jane Adams Postcard Collection in San Diego State University's Special Collections & University Archives (see page 127). The support from that department from the day I first proposed the project has been nothing but wonderful to receive. Thanks especially to Anna Culbertson and Amanda Lanthorne, as well as Sarah Conner, who is always pulling boxes of postcards for me.

All of the postcards in this book come from the John and Jane Adams Postcard Collection, San Diego State University Special Collections & University Archives.

INTRODUCTION

I met a traveller from an antique land
Who said: "Two vast and trunkless legs of stone
Stand in the desert. . . . Near them, on the sand,
Half sunk, a shattered visage lies, whose frown,
And wrinkled lip, and sneer of cold command,
Tell that its sculptor well those passions read
Which yet survive, stamped on these lifeless things,
The hand that mocked them, and the heart that fed;
And on the pedestal these words appear:
'My name is Ozymandias, king of kings;
Look on my works, ye mighty and despair!'
Nothing beside remains. Round the decay
Of that colossal wreck, boundless and bare
The lone and level sands stretch far away."

—Percy Bysshe Shelley, *Ozymandias*

California is indeed an antique land, and in many places, the lone and level sands stretch far away, and for many of the places in this book, not even two vast and trunkless legs of stone remain.

California was peopled by natives before the Spanish (in the form of Cabrillo in 1542) and the English (in the form of Drake in 1579) arrived. It took another two centuries before the Spanish missionaries moved north from Baja California into what they called Alta California. It was known as Alta California through the 1821 revolution that made it part of Mexico instead of Spain and finally became simply California when it was ceded to the United States as part of the Treaty of Guadalupe Hidalgo at the conclusion of the Mexican-American War in 1848. It had gained an aura of romance through the gold rush that made the population explode and has not stopped growing since. California, young by the standards of the East Coast, is filled with history. However, history can disappear as quickly as it was created, leaving only an image behind.

Emblematic of this change is San Diego Stadium. Or perhaps it is Jack Murphy Stadium. Or it might even be Qualcomm Stadium or SDCCU (San Diego County Credit Union) Stadium. All of these refer to the same building—or what was the same building, just with different names over time. That structure is now gone, as is one of the sports franchises that made it the team's home for decades (the San Diego Chargers, who abandoned their initial city for Los Angeles). Images of the stadium, however, remain. The past stays alive through images.

California has always had an indelible connection between its past and present. Snapdragon Stadium, which was built in 2021–22 and stands where San Diego Stadium once stood, is a short walk from Mission San Diego de Alcalá, a building that has existed since the early 18th century (the original mission was burned down long before the invention of postcards). The postcards in this collection bridge that connection.

No part of California has been spared from nature's fury. While the 1906 earthquake and fire that destroyed San Francisco is well-known, it is less commonly noted for the kind of damage it wrought upon Stanford University. The 1933 Long Beach earthquake took down other buildings, and the 1971 San Fernando earthquake made clear how many buildings in the state were still unsound and needed to be demolished. Fires have ravaged the state from Yosemite to Santa Cruz to Santa Barbara to Redondo Beach to San Diego. It sometimes seems that every classic hotel built in the state in the late 19th or early 20th century must have burned to the ground—except the Hotel del Coronado. Indeed, this book could have been a lot longer (or an entirely separate book) if it had solely featured hotels.

But nature is not the only bringer of the destruction that has been wrought upon the state and the beautiful sights it once held. Most of the buildings put up for the 1915 Panama-California Exhibition in San Diego's Balboa Park were not meant to last, and so they did not. Los Angeles decided, at one point, that Bunker Hill was an impediment to progress, so it leveled the hill after leveling the buildings upon it. There are postcards that represent the towns of Alma and Kennett, which readers may have never heard of because the state buried them under millions of gallons of water years ago during the construction of Shasta Lake and Lexington Reservoir.

Disneyland, Knott's Berry Farm, and Six Flags Magic Mountain have been entertaining people for decades. But long before any of these even broke ground, the state had an abundance of amusement parks. From Idora Park in Oakland to the Chutes in San Francisco to any number of competing waterfront parks in Los Angeles County, people were being entertained on rides before Walt Disney ever left Missouri.

Among the postcards in this book, you will find places that you never even knew were lost— sometimes right next to places that are still extant. California seems so awash in history, from the missions to Yosemite to Balboa Park's museums, that it can sometimes be difficult to remember that so much of it has been lost over time. However, even if the places themselves were lost, the images of those places still survive.

One

Municipal Buildings

City Hall, Anaheim, Cal.

The second Anaheim City Hall was constructed in 1892 and was torn down after the third one was constructed in 1923. Like many city halls of the era, it had a far more unique look to it than the current (fourth) hall, which was constructed in 1980. Anaheim is the largest city in Orange County in Southern California.

City Hall, Los Angeles, Cal.

After using many temporary locations since its incorporation in 1850, this building was the first city hall constructed exclusively for that use in the city of Los Angeles. It served as city hall from 1888 until the completion of the new building in 1928. The old city hall was demolished in 1928, and its former location became a parking lot.

This image of the Los Angeles County Hall of Records also offers an obstructed view of the Los Angeles County Courthouse in downtown Los Angeles. The courthouse was damaged in the 1933 Long Beach earthquake and was condemned and later demolished in 1936, with its replacement later being built in the same location. The Hall of Records was found to be structurally unsound after the 1971 San Fernando earthquake and was demolished in 1973.

Hall of Records and County Court House Los Angeles, Cal.

Hall of Records and Old City Hall, San Francisco, Cal.

These are two different views of the original San Francisco City Hall and Hall of Records in the space that is now UN Plaza. Completed in 1899 after 27 years of planning and construction, the first building lasted less than 7 years, as it was completely destroyed by the 1906 earthquake and fire, as shown below. The divided-back postcard above was produced no earlier than a year after the earthquake but shows the buildings before the devastation. The postcard below shows what the buildings looked like after the earthquake knocked them apart and the fire gutted what was left.

CITY HALL. SAN FR

In a 46-year span in the late 19th and early 20th centuries, Andrew Carnegie funded 1,689 libraries in the United States. The San Diego Public Library was the first Carnegie library in California when it opened in 1902. Over the next 50 years, as the population of San Diego increased exponentially, the library became too small to serve the city. After a bond issue passed in 1949, the library was demolished in 1952, with its replacement opening in the same location in 1954.

The Carnegie library located in Riverside, California (in California's Inland Empire, east of Los Angeles), on the corner of Seventh and Orange Streets, opened in 1903 and was designed by the firm of Burnham and Bleisner. After Carnegie-funded additions in 1908 and 1920, the library was demolished in 1964 after another building was opened. This German-made divided-back postcard dates from between 1907, when divided-back postcards began in the United States, and 1915, when war-induced tariffs essentially ended the large market in the United States for postcards produced in Germany.

Just 11 miles from the Riverside library, and also in the Inland Empire, was the San Bernardino library, another Carnegie library built by the firm of Burnham and Bleisner. It opened a year later than the Riverside library (in 1904), but it was demolished earlier (in 1958).

The Watsonville Public Library in downtown Watsonville in Central California was also a Carnegie library but was designed by William H. Weeks, a prominent Northern California architect whose first office was in Watsonville, although Weeks later moved to San Francisco. It opened in 1905 and was demolished in 1975 to make way for a new, larger building.

In 1892, when the second San Diego County Courthouse was determined to be unfit to have new wings added, it was demolished instead, and this third structure was built at the corner of Front and D (now Broadway) Streets. In 1961, in need of asbestos abatement and in a precarious location on the Rose Canyon Fault, this building was demolished. The 42 clerestory stained-glass windows were saved and sat in storage until 1996, when they were placed in the Hall of Justice that adjoined the new courthouse.

This courthouse with a clock tower was built in 1874 on Court Street in San Bernardino, damaged in the 1923 earthquake, and replaced in 1927. The information available from the Curt Teich Postcard Archives at Lake County Forest Preserves dates the card to 1915 by using its production number (A-61254).

The Los Angeles County Courthouse moved into this building at Temple Street and Broadway in 1891. The building, which was demolished in 1932, faced south and was next to the Hall of Records (built in 1906), which was on the left.

11465. Sonoma County Court House, Santa Rosa, Cal.

Built in 1907 to replace the courthouse that had been destroyed in the 1906 earthquake, this is the Sonoma County Courthouse in Santa Rosa, Northern California. It was deemed seismologically unsafe and razed in the mid-1960s.

Hollywood Library
Hollywood, Cal.

Established on February 8, 1906, by the Woman's Club of Hollywood, this building was on the corner of Prospect (now Hollywood) Boulevard and Ivar Avenue in 1907. The land was donated for this purpose, and the $15,000 construction was mostly funded by Andrew Carnegie for the one-story, English bungalow–style building. It was demolished in 1958. The John and Jane Adams Postcard Collection has over 20 different postcards addressed to Maude Bakewell among the California postcards alone. They help trace her life, following her move from St. Helena, California, to San Diego in late 1911 or early 1912, and the cards addressed to her range from 1906 to 1927. This particular card is postmarked September 19, 1921, and is from Maude's friend Allie.

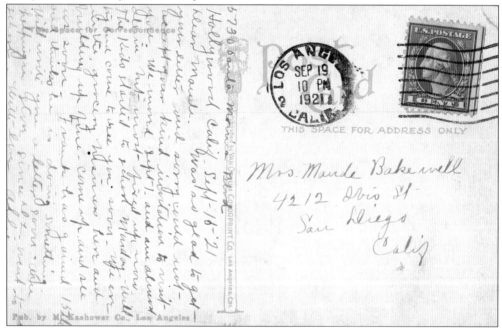

Until April 1907, postcards in the United States had undivided backs, which allowed space for the address of a recipient but no message. Cards of the period often had white space on the front for messages. This card featuring the Santa Clara County Courthouse and Hall of Records in San Jose contains ample writing around the margins. The Hall of Records, built in 1892, was demolished in 1962. The courthouse still stands, though it is not used for courtroom proceedings, and the dome was destroyed by fire in 1931.

The San Jose City Hall, dedicated in 1889, also housed the library and jail and was built at a cost of $140,000 in Plaza Park (now Plaza de Cesar Chavez) after the Chinatown plaza burned down in 1887. In spite of damage from the 1906 earthquake, it lasted until it was replaced in 1958.

This card shows the courthouse (built in 1889) and hall of records (built in 1909) for Shasta County in Redding in Northern California. The courthouse was demolished in 1963, and the hall followed in 1998.

SAN JOAQUIN COUNTY COURT HOUSE FROM HUNTER SQUARE, STOCKTON, CALIFORNIA.

The old San Joaquin County Courthouse sat in Hunter Square in Stockton in Central California. The courthouse was built in the late 19th century and was used by the county until 1930. It was demolished in 1961 to make room for the current courthouse. Teich No. A-65004 dates the card to 1916.

Two

CHURCHES

11492.   South Methodist Church, Santa Rosa, Cal.

The Methodist Episcopal Church South in Santa Rosa, California, was built in 1868 at the corner of Fifth and Orchard Streets near downtown. It had ceased to be a church by the time it was used as one in the 1943 Alfred Hitchcock film *Shadow of a Doubt*. The location is now home to a parking garage.

Dr. J. Whitcomb Brougher   The Auditorium, Home of the Temple Baptist Church, Los Angeles, Cal.   Dr. Robert J. Burdette

The Auditorium (exterior above, interior below) opened in 1906 across the street from Pershing Square in Los Angeles on the former site of Hazard's Pavilion, which had been famous for its boxing matches. Known as Clune's Auditorium and, later, Philharmonic Auditorium (after the Los Angeles Philharmonic Orchestra became a permanent resident in 1920), it had the largest stage west of New York and held 2,600 people. In the early 20th century, it was also home to the Temple Baptist Church. It was demolished in 1985.

The Interior of the Auditorium, Los Angeles, Cal.

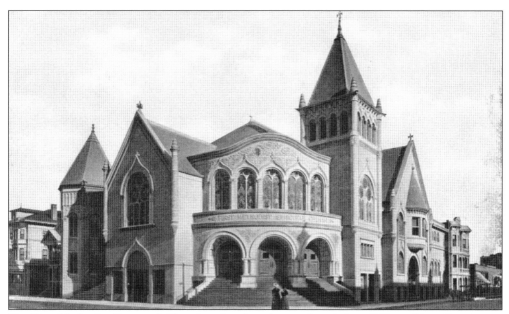

The First Methodist Episcopal Church in Los Angeles was founded in 1853 not long after the city was incorporated. In 1900, the church moved into this building on the corner of Eighth and Hope Streets in downtown Los Angeles. In the 1990s, with the building no longer meeting the needs of the congregation, it was torn down. The congregation continues to meet in a parking lot and does not currently have a permanent physical home.

The Christian Church Tabernacle was in the Garfield Park neighborhood of Santa Cruz, California. In the late 1880s, the Garfield Park neighborhood, named after former president James A. Garfield, was laid out in concentric circles around a central circle where the octagonal Christian Church Tabernacle was built and opened in 1890. The church burned down in 1935 and was replaced across the street. The replacement was closed in 1958 when a new building was erected in the original location. That building is now the Coryell Autism Center.

First Methodist Church, San Diego, Cal., Corner Ninth and C Streets

The First Methodist Church, built in 1906 to house a congregation founded in 1869, was said to be the first Protestant church in San Diego County. In subsequent times, it was known as the First Methodist Episcopal Church. Since 1964, this congregation has been located in Mission Valley on Camino del Rio South and known as the First United Methodist Church. This building at the corner of Ninth Avenue and C Street was later demolished, and the entire block is listed among the Save Our Heritage Organisation's "100 Lost Buildings" in San Diego. This undivided-back postcard dates from 1906, not long after the church was built.

Designed by William H. Weeks, who was a member of the congregation, the Christian church in Watsonville, California, was built in 1903 to replace a previous version (also designed by Weeks) and burned down in 1927.

Three

NATURAL SETTINGS

Firefall was a summertime event in Yosemite National Park that ran from 1872 to 1968. Glowing embers were raked over the top of Glacier Point by the owners of the Glacier Point Hotel. The National Park Service ordered that the event be stopped in 1968—not due to fear of fire, but because crowds were trampling the meadows to see it, and it was not considered a natural event. The Glacier Point Hotel burned down 18 months later. The event can still be seen on film in *The Caine Mutiny*, although, ironically, the event is depicted during World War II, when it was suspended.

YOSEMITE NATIONAL PARK

328   THE FIRE FALL, FROM GLACIER POINT   3A-H148

The Wawona Tunnel Tree stood in the Mariposa Grove in Yosemite National Park. It was 227 feet tall and had a base that was 27 feet in diameter. A tunnel was cut through the tree in 1881. The tree fell under the weight of snow in February 1969. Estimated to be over 2,300 years old, the tree still lies where it fell. Jane Adams, addressed here as Mrs. J.R. Adams, was married to John R. Adams from the early 1920s until his death in 1994. Together, they collected over 200,000 postcards, which can be found in the Special Collections & University Archives at San Diego State University. This card was postmarked to her from Yosemite's Camp Curry on July 2, 1955.

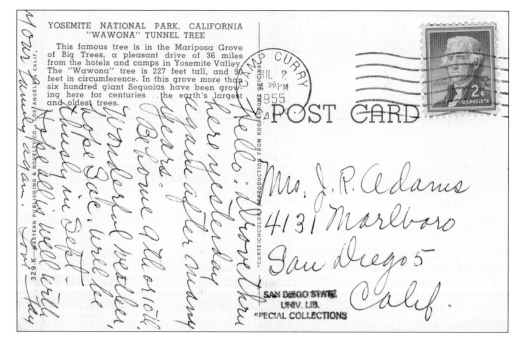

The Original Navel Orange Tree Planted in Riverside in 1873.

The tree enshrined here was also called the "Parent Washington Navel Orange Tree" on the plaque marking it as Historical Landmark No. 20 in the State of California. It was grown by Eliza Tibbets in Riverside in 1873 just as the orange industry was beginning to thrive in Southern California. This tree died in 1921.

"COOLIDGE TREE"

COOLIDGE TREE
Col. John Coolidge

F-162-C   COOLIDGE REDWOOD PARK ON THE REDWOOD HIGHWAY, IN CALIFORNIA

Tunneled through in the 1910s and dedicated to John Coolidge, father of former president Calvin Coolidge, the Coolidge Tree sat in Leggett in Northern California in Coolidge Redwood Park (later renamed Underwood Park and then Drive-Thru Tree Park). When it appeared to be failing in 1938, it was cut down, and a nearby tree was tunneled and named Chandelier Tree as a replacement tourist attraction. The Teich production number of 3A-H354 identifies the card as being from 1933.

4607. Sphinx Head Cave, La Jolla, near San Diego, Cal.

Depending on whether it was viewed looking north (above) or south (below), the same rock arch had two different names in the La Jolla neighborhood of San Diego. Whether it was known as Sphinx Head or Alligator Head, the arch collapsed during a winter storm in 1978. The rocks still exist in the water, but a fence keeps people from getting too close to what is now a cliff.

4614 Alligator Head, La Jolla, San Diego, Calif.

8A-H109

Crown Rock and Natural Arch - Santa Cruz, California

Crown Rock was a naturally-formed arch along the beach just west and north of the city of Santa Cruz in Central California. Due to strong waves and rocks that offer little resistance, this area of the California coast features many natural arches created by erosion that suddenly collapse later after more erosion. Crown Rock collapsed at some point in the mid-20th century.

THE TWIN NATURAL BRIDGES ALONG FAMOUS CLIFF DRIVE, SANTA CRUZ, CALIFORNIA

The Twin Natural Bridges were on the Central California coast near Santa Cruz. Like Crown Rock, they suffered from erosion problems over the years. The bridges collapsed at some point in the mid-20th century.

The Ostrich Tree was a tourist attraction along 17 Mile Drive, a tourist loop in Monterey County that covers the upper part of the Monterey Peninsula in Central California. Made from two cypress trees that had grown together, the tree was also known as the Lone Ostrich or Ostrich Trees and was widely photographed. It was blown down by a storm in 1906.

A breakwater starts in the foreground and stretches out to Deadman's Island, a landmark removed starting in 1928 as the Los Angeles Harbor expanded in San Pedro Bay. The jagged piles of stone date back to the mid-19th century. In his 19th-century work *Two Years Before the Mast*, Richard Henry Dana Jr. described the island, stating, "It was the only spot in California that impressed me with anything like poetic interest."

1411:—"The Witch Tree," Cypress on the 17 Mile Drive, Monterey Peninsula, Calif.

Like the Ostrich Tree (shown on the previous page), the Witch Tree was a famous cypress tree along 17 Mile Drive on the Monterey Peninsula. The Witch Tree lasted much longer, though, and was finally blown over during a storm on January 14, 1964.

136:—NATURAL ARCH, "CATHEDRAL" ROCK, NEAR SAN DIEGO, CALIF.

A natural rock arch on the shores of the La Jolla neighborhood of San Diego, Cathedral Rock (also called Cathedral Arch) collapsed between 3:00 and 4:00 on the morning of January 19, 1906. The individual rocks still stand in La Jolla Cove.

29

The Joseph Hooker Oak in Bidwell Park in Chico in Northern California was named after English botanist Joseph Hooker in 1877. It became famous through its appearance in the 1938 film *The Adventures of Robin Hood*. By the time the tree fell in 1977, it was nearly 100 feet tall.

The rock known as "the meteor" in Alum Rock Park in San Jose may not have been a meteor at all but rather just a rock outcropping. Opened in 1872, Alum Rock Park in San Jose is the oldest municipal park in California. Until the 1930s, it was a popular destination due to hot springs, but the meteor was broken up in 1918 so its materials could be used in World War I.

Four

URBAN SETTINGS

The Garden City Bank Building in downtown San Jose opened in 1908. At seven stories, it was the tallest building in San Jose. Starting in 1909, it was home to the Herrold College of Wireless and Engineering, the first school designed to teach radio engineers. It was demolished in 1987.

The Hotel Brewster in San Diego, shown on the corner of Fourth Avenue and C Street (with a sign near street level toward the right), operated from 1888 until 1934, when it was demolished. In the center of the street is a Class 1 streetcar with the enhanced sign "Ramonas Home, Pacific Beach, La Jolla" on the front and a horse and carriage approaching the camera in front of it. Class 1 (covered) streetcars with central entrances were introduced in 1912 after problems surfaced with the open California cars. The streetcar line to La Jolla was No. 16, and the full reach of the line to La Jolla was completed in 1924. The Class 1 San Diego streetcar was retired in 1939.

Construction began on the San Diego Naval Hospital in 1922 after a tent dispensary had been established in 1914. More land was deeded to the Navy in subsequent years, and finally, a new Naval Medical Center in Florida Canyon, located east of this complex, was dedicated in 1988. Only the front section in the center-right still remains from this original building.

The Long Beach Elks Lodge No. 888 is described on the back of this postcard as such: "The 4-inch-thick concrete dome of this spectacular building acts as ceiling and provides exceptionally good acoustics for the 1100-seat lodge room beneath it. In back is a vast patio, with swim pool, shuffleboard, bar-b-que and terrace." The complex was finished in 1963 and demolished by 2012.

The Markwell Building in Long Beach, later called the Jergins Trust Building, was opened in 1919 and demolished in 1988. It and the State Theatre inside were designed by architects Harvey H. Lochridge and Kirkland Cutter. Loew's, which has signs above the building on two sides, operated the theater from the late 1910s until around 1921.

The Paradise Valley Sanitarium opened in 1887 in National City, just south of San Diego. Lacking water and patients, it closed in 1895. In 1910, the building was sold to the Seventh-Day Adventist Church, which opened a school for nurses on the site in 1914. It moved locations in 1966, and today, all that remains of the original site are a gate and a bronze plaque noting the location.

This auditorium in Long Beach was built in 1932 and demolished in 1975. It was designed by J. Harold McDowell and extended 500 feet from the mainland at the center of the Rainbow Pier. The first auditorium (built in 1905) was demolished after this one opened. The Teich production number of 3A-H1378 dates this postcard to 1933.

Angel's Flight was a funicular railway that began operating in 1901 in the Bunker Hill district of downtown Los Angeles. The tracks connected Hill Street and Olive Street, with part of that run offering this view of downtown. The original location was closed and demolished in 1969, with a new location opened in 1996, but long before that, much of this view was demolished when Bunker Hill was leveled during construction in the 1950s.

This view looking north from the Call Building in downtown San Francisco at the corner of Market and Third Streets predates the widespread destruction caused by the 1906 earthquake and fire, and much of what is shown here was destroyed. After the earthquake, the *San Francisco Call* moved to another building, and the structure was renamed the Spreckels Building.

Grosse Building, Los Angeles, Cal.

The Grosse Building, formerly the Abbot Kinney, was completed in 1906 on the southeast corner of Sixth and Spring Streets in Los Angeles. The building was home to the Southern Pacific Railroad. It was demolished in 1958. This is a German-produced divided-back postcard, which limits the production to sometime between 1907 and 1915.

This building was completed in 1908 in the Classical Revival style and stood on the southeast corner of Eleventh and Main Streets in Riverside. It was sold to the Elks Club in 1916, which held it until 1956, when the club moved. In 1959, it was demolished.

The Wyatt Theatre opened in 1904 as the Wyatt Opera House in Redlands in California's Inland Empire. It was closed in 1928 and demolished in 1929 for safety reasons. The Teich production number of A-9283 marks this card as being from 1910.

On this card, a two-story building with a false front stands on a corner with both automobiles and horse-drawn vehicles in the streets. The Contemporary Club was a women's club organized in 1894 that joined the California Federation of Women's Clubs in 1900. This 1904 building stood at the southeast corner of Vine and Fourth Streets in Redlands in the Inland Empire and was designed by Arthur B. Benton in a combination of Mission Revival and Tudor (half-timber) styles. It was demolished in 1971.

ALHAMBRA THEATRE. SACRAMENTO, CALIFORNIA   3994-29

The Alhambra Theatre in Sacramento was constructed in 1927. Located in the East Sacramento neighborhood, it was the preeminent movie theater in the Sacramento area until was demolished in 1973. It is now a Safeway supermarket. The Teich production number of 3994-29 dates this card to 1929.

"City of Paris,"
San Francisco

The City of Paris Dry Goods Company in San Francisco is pictured here from across the street in Union Square. Founded in 1850, the building was one of the few in the neighborhood to survive the 1906 earthquake and fire that destroyed the city. It was a Beaux-Arts building designed by architect Clinton Day. The store closed in 1972, and the building was sold to Neiman Marcus in 1974, which demolished it in 1981 and built a new store in its place.

The Orpheum and Princess Theatres were next to each other on Ellis Street in San Francisco. The Princess opened as a vaudeville theater in 1907, after the 1906 earthquake left downtown ravaged and many events moved to the Fillmore. The Princess became the Ellis in 1935, closed in 1952, and was demolished in the 1970s. The Orpheum was renamed the Garrick in 1909 and lasted through the 1920s, becoming a bowling alley in the 1930s (and, later, a church) before it was demolished in the 1970s.

This building on Market Street in San Francisco housed three stores. It also marked the home of Serwe & Prien Co. According to the back of the card, it was a "druggists' sundries and manufacturer's agents." The building, which was located right in the heart of downtown, no longer exists.

On the left is the Hotel St. Mark, for which ground was broken in 1904. It was one of the original buildings in Venice before it was annexed by Los Angeles in 1925. The hotel, which took up about a block of the originally two-block-long town, was demolished in 1964. Venice once stretched from the lagoon (at the location that later became home to the traffic circle at Windward Circle and Main Street) to the Abbot Kinney Pier.

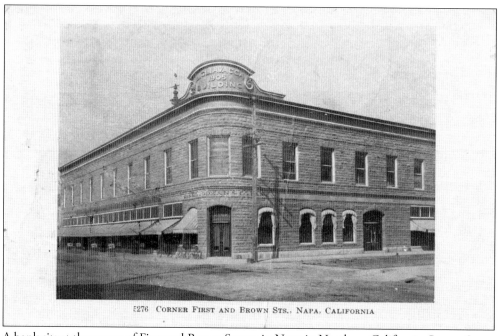

£276 CORNER FIRST AND BROWN STS., NAPA, CALIFORNIA

A bank sits at the corner of First and Brown Streets in Napa in Northern California. Brown Street no longer connects with First Street; a pedestrian mall filled in that portion of the street.

The nine-story Montgomery Ward & Company Building in the Fruitvale neighborhood of Oakland was the largest industrial building in the city when it was erected in 1923. It functioned as both a store (on the bottom two floors) and a warehouse. The building was demolished in 2000.

Oakland, Cal., Central Bank Building.

The Central Bank Building in Oakland was originally constructed in 1893. The five-story building was damaged in the 1906 earthquake and was torn down in 1925 after the bank outgrew it. A new building, which still stands, replaced it in 1926. The presence of First Presbyterian Church of Oakland on the far right dates the card to sometime before 1914, when the church moved to a different address.

This postcard looks down Market Street in San Francisco before the 1906 earthquake and fire. On the left is the Call Building (now Central Tower), the home of *the San Francisco Call* and, from 1898 to 1922, the tallest building not only in San Francisco but west of the Mississippi. It was mostly gutted but remained standing after the fire. Writing is on the bottom of the card, as it has an undivided back with no room for a message.

San Francisco, California. Sky Scrapers. Withstood earthquake, but succumbed to fire Apr. 18, 1906.

This card depicts Market Street in San Francisco between Third and Fourth Streets. Though this card, with a divided back, was produced no earlier than April 1907, the scene depicted is what Market Street looked like in 1905, before it was devastated by the 1906 earthquake and fire that destroyed much of the city.

Market St. betw. 3 d. & 4 th. St. Aug. 1905, San Francisco, Cal.

MARKET STREET BY NIGHT,
SHOWING PANTAGES AND EMPRESS THEATRE,
SAN FRANCISCO, CAL.

Featured prominently on the south side of Market Street between Fifth and Sixth Streets in San Francisco are the Pantages Theatre and the Empress Theatre. The Pantages closed in 1926, when its new, larger theater opened at 1192 Market Street. The building that housed the older Pantages housed retail establishments until its eventual demolition in 2013. The Teich production number of A-33523 dates this card to 1913.

The original building of the M.H. de Young Memorial Museum in Golden Gate Park in San Francisco was constructed for the California Midwinter International Exposition of 1894. The museum opened in 1895. After damage in the 1906 earthquake and a collection that no longer fit, the pictured building was condemned in 1929, but a new wing had opened in 1921 and continued as the main museum building. The second building closed in 2000, and a third building opened in 2005.

The San Jose Safe Deposit Bank Building was on the corner of First and Santa Clara Streets in downtown San Jose. The building was constructed in 1885 and demolished in 1925. The phrase "On the Road of a Thousand Wonders" (on the front of the card) was the slogan of the Southern Pacific Railroad and can be found on hundreds of postcards in the John and Jane Adams Postcard Collection.

The Mason Opera House in Los Angeles was on Broadway between First and Second Streets. Benjamin Marshall, of the firm Marshall and Wilson of Chicago, designed the Mason Opera House in association with prominent Los Angeles architect John Parkinson. In 1920, it was sold and became the Mason Theatre. It closed in 1955 and was demolished later that year.

Five

HOTELS AND RESTAURANTS

MOUNTAIN BROOK THROUGH DINING ROOM — BROOKDALE LODGE   BROOKDALE, CALIF.

The Brook Room in the Brookdale Lounge, north of Santa Cruz in Central California, combined nature and commerce. This dining room was designed by Horace Cotton—at the request of hotel owner F.K. Camp—to have the creek run through the center of the room. From the 1920s, when the Brook Room was designed, until October 1956, when it was destroyed in a fire, the lodge was famed for its Hollywood visitors, politicians, and mobsters. The back of the card, which identifies Camp as the owner of the hotel, dates it to between 1922 and 1945, when Camp owned the lodge.

THE SAN DIEGO HOTEL. ON BROADWAY   BUILT BY JOHN D. SPRECKELS

The San Diego Hotel was designed by Harrison Albright (1866–1932) for John D. Spreckels (1853–1926), a San Diego entrepreneur and civic leader. Built in 1914 for the Panama-California International Exposition of 1915, it closed in 2001 and was demolished in 2006 despite being listed as San Diego Historical Site No. 175 in 1983. Like many old hotels in San Diego, in its later years, it provided low-income housing.

The Hotel Balboa was built in 1888 as the principal building of the San Diego College of Letters at Pacific Beach. It was the first significant structure in Pacific Beach and was designed by James W. Reid, architect of the Hotel del Coronado. It became a hotel after the college failed in 1891. It later became part of Brown Military Academy but closed in 1958 and was demolished not long after; the location is now a shopping center.

Above is an aerial view of Tent City in Coronado, California, looking south along the Silver Strand in San Diego Bay. Until 1939, Tent City was an extension of the grounds of the Hotel del Coronado that offered cheaper accommodations than the hotel itself. Below, crowds flock along the boardwalk at Tent City's bathing pavilion.

Seventh Street Entrance to Los Angeles Ambassador

The Ambassador Hotel in Los Angeles was built on Wilshire Boulevard in 1921 and designed by Pasadena architect Myron Hunt. It became known as the home of the Cocoanut Grove nightclub and the hotel where Robert Kennedy was assassinated in 1968. It closed around 1988 and was demolished around 2006.

Hotel Statler on fabulous Wilshire Boulevard, Los Angeles, California   Ted Lewy ©71

In an illustration signed by Ted Lewy, the Statler Center (as it is referred to in a statement on the back of the card) rises into the sky at the corner of Wilshire Boulevard and Figueroa Street. It is described as the first Statler Hotel west of the Mississippi, with guest rooms, an office building, and shops on a four-acre site. It opened in 1952 and went through several name changes before demolition began in 2012 on what was, by that time, the Wilshire Grand Hotel.

THE ARLINGTON HOTEL, SANTA BARBARA, CAL.

This California Mission–style hotel designed by Arthur Benton stretches across the card in a three-quarter view from the entrance on the left to a turret on a wing on the right. It occupied the block bounded by Victoria, State, Sola, and Chapala Streets in Santa Barbara. The first wooden version of the Arlington Hotel burned in 1909, and the tower shown in this structure was destroyed in the 1925 earthquake when the water tank at the top collapsed. The Arlington Theater was built on the site after the hotel was razed in 1931. The Teich production number of A-66323 dates the card to 1916.

Hotel Hollywood at Hollywood, Cal.

The Hotel Hollywood (also called the Hollywood Hotel after the 1920s) was located on Hollywood Boulevard. The land for it was purchased in 1902. This is the expanded four-story structure, with renovations that began in 1905 and lasted until 1910. The structure was demolished in 1956. This German-produced divided-back postcard was made between 1907 and 1915.

49

Key Route Electric Trains to and from San Francisco every 15 Minutes at our door under cover.

Rear View KEY ROUTE INN - Oakland's Refined Hotel, showing Gardens adjoining and Children's Playgrounds. 1998

This page features a rear view of the Key Route Inn in Oakland (above) and a view of the front on Grand Avenue (below). It opened in 1907 and was torn down in 1932 after suffering major fire damage on September 8, 1930. The inn was built to service the Key System, the privately owned mass-transit system that prevailed in the East Bay from 1903 to 1960.

KEY ROUTE INN, OAKLAND, CAL.

The First Cliff House, destroyed by fire in 1894. San Francisco.

Three different restaurants in the northwest corner of San Francisco, on the cliff above Seal Rocks, have been called Cliff House. The first one, pictured above, was built in 1863 and burned down on Christmas night in 1894. The second Cliff House, pictured below, is shown on September 7, 1907, during the fire that destroyed it. The second one had been built by Adolph Sutro, who owned the nearby baths. The third Cliff House still stands.

Complete Destruction of Cliff House by Fire. S.F. Sept. 7. 1907.

OLD WASHINGTON HOTEL, MONTEREY, FIRST HOTEL IN CALIFORNIA

The Old Washington Hotel, located on Washington Street in Monterey, was the first hotel in California. It was built in 1832 and torn down in 1914 or 1915.

SEA BEACH HOTEL, THE POPULAR SEASIDE RESORT, SANTA CRUZ, CALIFORNIA

The Sea Beach Hotel, a Victorian-style hotel in Santa Cruz, was built in the 1870s by S.A. Hall. It originally opened as the Ocean View House and was renamed the Douglas House when it was sold in 1882 and then the Sea Beach Hotel when it was sold in 1886. The hotel burned to the ground in 1912. It covered the area bordered by Beach Street, Drift Way, Main Street, and Second Street and was located directly across the street from the Santa Cruz Wharf.

The Metropole Hotel was across Crescent Avenue from the Steamer Pier in Avalon on Catalina Island from 1887 to 1915. This card could have been produced at any time between March 31, 1907, when postal regulations changed to allow divided backs (like this one has) on postcards, and November 1915, when it burned down along with between one third and one half of the town of Avalon.

HOTEL
VENDOME

SAN JOSE
CALIFORNIA

The Hotel Vendome in San Jose was located north of downtown. It opened in 1889 and was demolished in 1930 for a residential neighborhood. A three-story annex built in 1903 was destroyed in the 1906 San Francisco earthquake.

Above is the exterior of the Hotel St. Catherine in Avalon on Catalina Island, and below is the dining room of the hotel. Construction started on the hotel in 1917 to replace the Metropole in Avalon, which was destroyed by a fire in 1915. By 1918, it was open for business, but when the island was bought by William Wrigley Jr. in 1919, a series of upgrades were made to the hotel, which ended in the early 1920s. It was demolished in 1966. The Teich production number of the above card, A-91772, indicates that it dates to 1922.

Virginia Hotel, Long Beach, Cal.

Above is a view from the road of the Virginia Hotel in Long Beach, and below is the hotel's staircase. Designed by architects John C. Austin and Frederick C. Brown, the Virginia Hotel was originally the Bixby Hotel but was renamed in 1906 and opened in 1908. It closed in 1932 after the stock-market crash, and it was demolished after the 1933 Long Beach earthquake.

Grand Stairway, Hotel Virginia, Long Beach, Calif.

The Hotel Redondo opened in 1890. The Victorian-style hotel with 225 rooms was a big enough draw that train lines were built out from Los Angeles to Redondo Beach to service the hotel, but Prohibition caused a serious decline. It was purchased by the city in 1922 and used for offices; it was dismantled in 1925.

Named after its owner Milo Potter, the Hotel Potter in Santa Barbara opened in 1903 as a year-round hotel (rather than a seasonal one) with accommodations for over 1,000 guests. It was sold in 1919, becoming the Belvedere, and then sold again, after which it became the Ambassador. In 1921, the hotel burned to the ground, and it was not rebuilt. Ambassador Park on West Cabrillo Boulevard is located at the former site of the hotel's entrance.

The Glacier Point Hotel opened on top of Glacier Point in 1918 with a view of Yosemite Valley. Hotel employees would rake embers off the point to create the nightly Firefall, which was visible from the valley floor. Snows damaged the hotel in the winter of 1968–69, and it was destroyed in a fire in July 1969.

The Hotel Anacapa was on a corner of Main and Palm Streets in Ventura in Southern California. It was built in 1888 by Fridolin Hartman and demolished in the 1920s. This postcard, printed in Germany, was produced between 1907 and 1915.

Noah's Ark was a restaurant in the beach town of Encinitas in northern San Diego County. It opened in 1946 and was known for the cutouts of animals that populated the hill behind the ark-shaped restaurant. It was demolished in the 1960s.

The Reuben E. Lee was a riverboat restaurant on Harbor Island in San Diego Bay. It offered a view of the bay and city to its diners for decades. It closed in 2004, and the riverboat sank on December 11, 2012.

A line of people waits to enter the Cabrillo, popularly known as the "Ship Café," built by Baron Long at Abbot Kinney's pier. The back of the card states: "This is the most unique cafe in America. Built after the design of the old Spanish caravels of the seventeenth century." Not only was the restaurant built to look like Juan Cabrillo's Spanish galleon, but the staff wore appropriate costumes. The establishment was also a hotel. It was removed sometime in the mid-20th century.

The Wagon Wheel Dance Hall was in Santee in eastern San Diego County in the days before highways made it a suburb of the city. It opened in 1944 and closed in 1976.

Kennett was a prosperous mining town in Northern California in the 19th century, but after the mine closed in 1923, the population fell so severely that the city was disincorporated in 1931. The Diamond Cafe, like everything else in the town, was lost in 1944 when it was submerged under Shasta Lake. The town currently sits in the deepest part of the lake, with not even severe droughts lowering the water level enough to have the remnants of the town break the surface.

The Delmonico in Southern California did not have the same level of fame as the New York restaurant of the same name, but it was an establishment in downtown Los Angeles in the first half of the 20th century. It was demolished in the 1950s, when downtown was remodeled.

Lucca Restaurant trumpeted its claim of being "famous the world over for fine food." A cookbook published by the restaurant in 1938 included numerous recipes from the establishment. It was on the corner of Fifth Street and Western Avenue in Los Angeles but gone by the late 20th century.

Clifton's Seas opened in 1931 on Olive Street near Pershing Square in Los Angeles and became a tiki bar in 1939. The restaurant, with a philosophy of "pay what you wish," was famous for not turning away those who could not pay. There were eventually eight locations, widely known as Clifton's Cafeteria, but this was the original location (with the exterior shown above and the interior shown below), although it was less well-known than the later downtown Los Angeles location at Seventh Street and Broadway, which survived until 2018. The original restaurant closed in 1960 and was razed; it is now a parking lot.

Aloha– Clifton's "Pacific Seas"
618 So. Olive St., Los Angeles

Clifton's Pacific Seas was so known for its kitschy atmosphere that NPR produced a 2006 article on the restaurant entitled, "Clifton's Cafeteria, Serving Kitsch Since 1935." The grotto area of the garden in the restaurant added to this atmosphere.

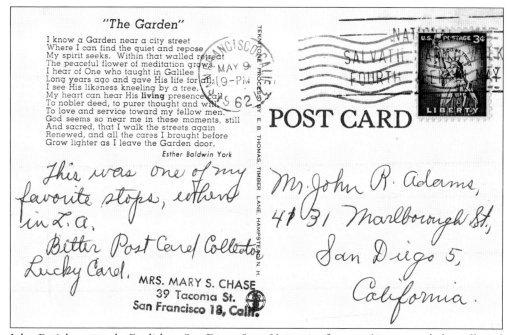

"The Garden"

I know a Garden near a city street
Where I can find the quiet and repose
My spirit seeks. Within that walled retreat
The peaceful flower of meditation grows.
I hear of One who taught in Galilee
Long years ago and gave His life for all;
I see His likeness kneeling by a tree.
My heart can hear His **living** presence call
To nobler deed, to purer thought and will,
To love and service toward my fellow men.
God seems so near me in these moments, still
And sacred, that I walk the streets again
Renewed, and all the cares I brought before
Grow lighter as I leave the Garden door.

Esther Baldwin York

POST CARD

This was one of my favorite stops, eithers in L.A. Better Post Card Collector. Lucky Card.

MRS. MARY S. CHASE
39 Tacoma St.
San Francisco 18, Calif.

Mr. John R. Adams,
4131 Marlborough St,
San Diego 5,
California.

John R. Adams taught English at San Diego State University for over 40 years and also collected over 200,000 postcards, which he donated to the school's Special Collections & University Archives after he became its first archivist. This postcard, addressed to Adams, was postmarked May 9, 1962, after Clifton's had already closed.

HOTEL BARBARA WORTH, EL CENTRO, CALIFORNIA

113315

The Hotel Barbara Worth opened in 1915 in El Centro in Imperial County in Southern California. It was the namesake of a fictional character created by Harold Bell Wright, whose *The Winning of Barbara Worth* was a bestseller. Wright, who lived near El Centro at the time, posed with one of the four murals on the lobby walls (below) by Edouard Vysekal and Luvena Buchanan, which were destroyed when the hotel burned down in 1962. Local citizens were used as models for the murals.

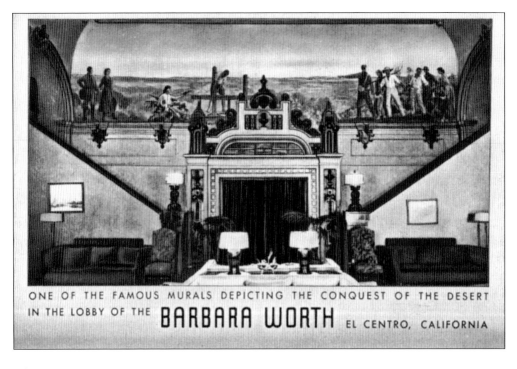

ONE OF THE FAMOUS MURALS DEPICTING THE CONQUEST OF THE DESERT IN THE LOBBY OF THE BARBARA WORTH EL CENTRO, CALIFORNIA

Six

SCHOOLS

183 Palo Alto, California, Entrance to the Stanford University.

The original entrance gates to Stanford University have never been replaced. Because it has a divided back, this postcard cannot have been produced before April 1907, but the image itself dates to no later than April 1906, as these gates were completely destroyed in the 1906 San Francisco earthquake.

185 Palo Alto, California, Leland Standford jr. University Library.

While much of the publicity of the 1906 earthquake focused on San Francisco, Stanford University was also badly damaged. The library, which had just been completed in 1900, was utterly destroyed. These postcards offer views from before (above) and after (below) the earthquake. The university was in such bad shape after the earthquake that it sent students home for the remainder of the quarter.

COPYRIGHT, 1906, BY AMERICAN-JOURNAL-EXAMINER.   RUINS OF STANFORD UNIVERSITY LIBRARY.

The Memorial Church at Stanford also
suffered heavy damage in the 1906
earthquake. The tower (shown above)
had only been completed in 1903,
and when the church was rebuilt after
the massive damage (depicted on the
postcard at right), the tower was not
included. The new church was not
completed until 1917 and was refitted
after it again suffered damage in the
1989 Loma Prieta earthquake.

The Altar in Stanford Memorial. Totally destroyed by Earthquake.
April 18th, 1906.

The First United Methodist Church in Escondido in northern San Diego County stands to the left of Escondido High School. Both of them were located near what is now downtown. A new high school opened in 1927 to ease overcrowding, and the original building burned down in 1929. The church was demolished in 1964 to make way for a new, larger church in the same location.

Petaluma High School was built in 1915 and designed by Brainerd Jones. This was the third high school in Petaluma in Sonoma County in Northern California. It was razed in 1958 to make way for a new high school.

The original building of Stockton High School in Central California was constructed in 1904 but became part of Stockton Junior High School in 1948 and was later deemed unsafe and demolished in 1967. The site is now the location of Commodore Stockton Junior High School.

The first Santa Rosa High School was completed in 1895 but destroyed by a fire in 1921. This location is currently the site of Santa Rosa Charter School for the Arts.

Paso Robles Grammar School was located just north of downtown Paso Robles in San Luis Obispo County in Central California. The school burned down in 1953. Today, the location is the home of Bauer Speck Elementary School.

Grant Grammar School (now Lowell Elementary School) was located north of downtown San Jose. This two-story school was constructed to replace a building destroyed by the 1906 earthquake and demolished in the 1970s due to heightened earthquake safety standards.

LONGFELLOW SCHOOL, SAN JOSE, CAL.

Longfellow School in San Jose, California, was a two-story school built to replace a previous school that had been destroyed in the 1906 earthquake. It was torn down in the 1970s due to substandard earthquake safety standards, and its students were transferred to Hester Elementary School. The school's former location is now a vacant lot.

1766- Horace Mann School, San Jose, California.

The Horace Mann School was built in 1907 to replace the Santa Clara Street School in San Jose, which had been destroyed in the 1906 earthquake. Like the Longfellow School, it was also torn down in the 1970s after it failed to meet earthquake safety standards. Students met in portable buildings for years until Horace Mann Elementary School opened in the same location in 2003.

State Normal School, San Diego, Cal.

What later became San Diego State University started as the State Normal School of San Diego in 1897. After a year in temporary accommodations in downtown San Diego, the main building was erected in the University Heights neighborhood north of Balboa Park. Dedicated in 1899, this structure was designed by Irving Gill (1870–1936), and construction continued to add on to it until 1910. In 1923, the name of the school was changed to San Diego State Teachers College. The college moved to Montezuma Mesa in 1931, and the original building was demolished in 1955. The site is now the home of the San Diego Public Schools administration. The Teich production number of A-29443 dates this card to 1911.

Normal School from Mission Cliff Park, San Diego, Cal.

While the State Normal School is in the background, in the foreground is Mission Cliff Park. Mission Cliff Park or Gardens, as it was also known, was a creation of the San Diego Cable Railway Company, owned by John D. Spreckels (1853–1926). It was in existence from 1898 to 1942 and was the original destination of the pipe organ that became the center of the Spreckels Organ Pavilion in Balboa Park and included an ostrich farm and an aviary. The Teich production number of A-13966 dates the postcard to 1910.

The training school was an integral part of San Diego State Teachers College. It had begun in 1900, and in 1910, a separate building was completed for the elementary school, where students at San Diego State could teach actual elementary-level students. In 1931, the school relocated to Montezuma Mesa, with the training school moving into this building. In 1935, San Diego State Teachers College became San Diego State College. In 1953, the training school was again relocated to a new building east of the Open Air Theatre. While this building still exists (and is now called Physical Sciences), the view is now blocked by several other structures, and the school no longer hosts an elementary school to train teachers.

Student Union

Photography: Ed Royce

San Diego State College's student union (called the Aztec Center) was built in 1968. The back of the card lists the school as San Diego State College, meaning that it was produced before July 1, 1972, when the school took on the short-lived name of Cal State University, San Diego. On January 1, 1974, it assumed the name it is still known by: San Diego State University. The Aztec Center was razed in 2011, and the Conrad Prebys Aztec Student Union now stands in its place.

The original San Diego High School was finished in 1882, and it burned down in 1911. It was replaced by this Gothic Revival building known as the Grey Castle and designed by F.S. Allen (1860–1934), with construction starting in 1906. Construction continued beyond this original building, with cornerstones for others laid in 1912, the stadium built in 1914, separate gymnasiums built for men and women in 1922 and 1923, and an auditorium built in 1926. After California legislation in the 1960s required the razing of all school buildings erected prior to 1933 due to earthquake concerns, architect Richard G. Wheeler (1917–1990) was retained in 1970 to design a new school. Demolition and construction proceeded simultaneously on different buildings; it started in 1973 and ended with the occupation of all four new buildings in 1977.

Hollywood High School is located on the corner of Sunset Boulevard and Highland Avenue in Hollywood. It opened in 1903 and moved into this building in 1904, when Hollywood was still a separate incorporated city and not a neighborhood of Los Angeles. It has a close connection to the film community of Hollywood, serving as the location for many films and television shows and the alma mater for a large number of actors. By the 1950s, the pictured building was the administration building; it was razed after the 1971 San Fernando earthquake.

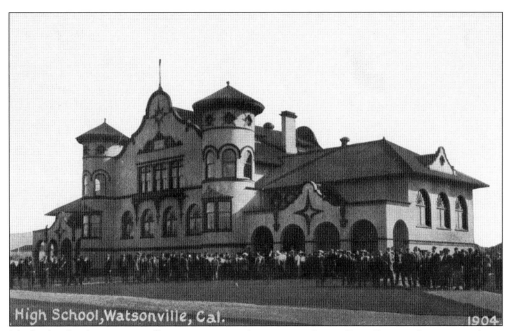

The high school in Watsonville was constructed in 1902 in Santa Cruz County. It was torn down in 1964 to make way for a new, larger school in the same location.

This is the original building for Coronado High School. It was constructed in 1913 and torn down in 1938 to be replaced by a Works Progress Administration building. That building was torn down in December 1960 because of earthquake concerns. Coronado sits on the peninsula in San Diego Bay. The Teich production number of A-57816 dates this card to 1915.

This hall on the campus of the University of California, Berkeley, was built by Phoebe Apperson Hearst for entertaining. It was next to her house at Piedmont Avenue and Channing Way, which was designed by Bernard Maybeck. She had it moved to College Avenue north of Bancroft Way and then remodeled as a gymnasium, with it becoming Hearst Hall for Women. Hearst gave the building and land to the university in 1899; an annex was added in 1901, and a fire destroyed the building in 1922. This divided-back card was produced in Germany, limiting its years of potential production to sometime between 1907 and 1915.

Hearst Memorial Mining Building was completed in 1907 on the campus of the University of California, Berkeley. A gift of Phoebe Apperson Hearst, it was designed by John Galen Howard (assisted by Julia Morgan) and named after Sen. George Hearst. The Mechanics Building (center), as it was called until 1931, was designed by William Curlett and finished in 1893. It was known as the Mechanical and Electrical Engineering Building from 1931 until it was demolished in 1965.

The Bacon Art and Library Building, shown here covered with ivy and behind a hedge, was next to the site of Sather Tower on the campus of the University of California, Berkeley. After its name was changed to Bacon Hall in 1911, it remained in use until 1961, when it was razed to clear the site for Birge Hall. This postcard dates from the early period of divided backs, when a message was still not allowed to be written on the back, so the white space at the bottom of the card was designed to allow for the sender to write a message there.

The Chemistry Building at the University of California, Berkeley, was designed by Clinton Day and completed in 1891, with additions made in 1901, 1902, and 1912. It was razed around 1966 to clear the site for Hildebrand Hall.

Real-photo postcards were popular from the 1930s to the 1950s. They allowed tourists to take a picture on a special type of film and have it developed as a postcard. This is a real-photo postcard of Rio Vista Joint Union High School (now Rio Vista High School) in Rio Vista in Solano County in Northern California. This building was constructed in 1915 and torn down in the 1960s, with new buildings erected in the same location.

Banning High School was a Mission-style, one-story brick building with two wings and a central entrance area. The 1933 Long Beach earthquake made the city realize it was unsafe, and it was replaced in 1938 with the current cement building, which opened in 1939 in the same location. Banning is in Southern California in the Inland Empire area east of Los Angeles.

Seven

TRANSPORTATION

The Great Incline at Mount Lowe, north of Los Angeles, was the opening stage of the Mount Lowe Railway. Designed to give people in the Los Angeles area an impressive view without having to spend all day climbing Mt. Wilson, the railway opened in 1893. It was abandoned in 1938 after years of declining revenue.

Once at the top of the Great Incline (pictured on the previous page), people could ride the Mount Lowe Railway itself—the only overhead scenic mountain electric trolley built in the United States. Like the incline, the railway was abandoned in 1938, though parts of its ruin can still be seen on the mountain today.

Billed as "the crookedest railroad in the world" to match Lombard Street, "the crookedest street in the world," in nearby San Francisco, the Mt. Tamalpais Railway opened in 1896. Though it was popular for over 30 years, a 1929 fire and a road that allowed automobiles to reach the top of the mountain doomed the railway, and it closed in 1930.

The incline railway Island Mountain Railway on Catalina Island ran from the top of the amphitheater in Avalon up the mountain to an inn at the top. The incline railway on the other side was called Angel's Flight and led to Pebbly Beach, making it a rare double-sided funicular. It ran from 1904 to 1918 and then again from 1921 until it permanently closed in 1923. The Teich production number of A-12562 marks the date of the card's production to 1910.

Capitola, located just east of Santa Cruz in Central California, has no Main Street, but pictured here is the esplanade with the Capitola Hotel in the background. A trolley rides streetcar lines across the boardwalk from the beach. This is the only location where houses are at the same level as the beach in such proximity. The postcard dates no later than 1926, when streetcar service ended in the area.

Longest Wharf in the World, Port Los Angeles, Cal.

This 4,600-foot wharf, located a half mile north of Santa Monica Canyon, entered into the Free Harbor Fight that led to the selection of the Port of Los Angeles in San Pedro Bay in 1897. The Free Harbor Fight pitted US senator Stephen M. White against railroad baron Collis Huntington, owner of the Southern Pacific Railroad. White resisted pressure from Huntington to make Santa Monica the official Port of Los Angeles, and the harbor was eventually awarded to San Pedro. The view to the left looks at it straight on from the land, while the below image shows it from farther south, looking north. This pier was named Port Los Angeles and jutted into Santa Monica Bay from what became Pacific Palisades. After losing the Free Harbor Fight, the wharf was closed to shipping in 1913 and torn down by 1920.

Port Los Angeles from the Pallisades, Santa Monica, Cal.

The Southern Pacific Terminus was in the SoMa (South of Market) neighborhood of San Francisco. The terminus was torn down in the 1970s. This card was one of 18 paper interior postcards in a series of 20 interconnected foldout postcards of San Francisco designed to be sent as an intact book. The set dates from the late 1920s or early 1930s, after the first wave of skyscrapers in San Francisco but before the construction of the San Francisco–Oakland Bay Bridge.

Central Station in Los Angeles was also known as Southern Pacific Depot because it was the main western terminus for Southern Pacific Railroad for its entire existence. Opened in 1914, the depot closed in 1939, when Union Station opened to consolidate the various railways in Los Angeles. The Teich production number of A-61514 dates the card to 1915.

R.-62. Highway Bridge across Santa Ana River, Riverside, Calif.

The Rubidoux Bridge in Needles, on the outskirts of the Inland Empire, had Mission Revival–style portals and was in use from 1923 until 1958, when it was replaced. This view antedates the widening of the bridge in 1931. One of the portals shown here survives on the east bank along what became a bicycle trail. The Teich production number of 95063 dates the card to 1923.

R. R. Bridge at Needles, Cal.

This image shows the Red Rock Bridge that joins San Bernardino County, California, to Mojave County, Arizona. The cantilevered-through-truss bridge was built in 1890 and became an automobile highway (Route 66) in 1947. It was replaced in 1966 and demolished in 1978. This divided-back postcard was produced in Germany, limiting the date of production to sometime between 1907 and 1915.

84

These three people posed on a pedestrian bridge over the San Lorenzo River. They are in Henry Cowell Redwoods State Park (formerly Big Tree Grove), a state park in the Santa Cruz Mountains just north of Santa Cruz in Central California. This was one of several bridges over the river that were all gone by 1955, when the last one was destroyed by a flood.

The Carquinez Bridge crossed the Carquinez Strait northeast of San Francisco. Completed in 1927, the bridge was the first to cross any substantial portion of the San Francisco Bay Area and rerouted the Lincoln Highway to travel directly from Sacramento to the East Bay. The original 1927 bridge was demolished in 2007. The Teich production number of 154-29 dates the card to 1929.

Stone Bridge, Alma, Calif.

No. 2801. Publ. Atlas Society 10. E. 23. St. New York. Made in Germany.

California has its share of ghost towns, but Alma is much rarer, in that it is a drowned town. In 1952, Alma and nearby Lexington were submerged when Lexington Reservoir was created above Los Gatos, south of San Jose. In times of low water, parts of Alma occasionally resurface. One cement bridge resurfaced in 2008, when the reservoir was at 7 percent capacity, but that cement bridge had an engraved date of 1926, and this divided-back postcard of a stone bridge was printed in Germany between 1907 and 1915.

Salt Lake R. R. Bascule Bridge, Long Beach, Cal.
Largest of its kind in the world.

This bridge, later replaced by the Henry Ford Bridge, joined Terminal Island in San Pedro Harbor to the mainland of Long Beach by rail. It displaced an earlier fixed bridge so that ships could pass through the channel using a bascule design by Joseph Strauss that was based on medieval drawbridges. This early tinted postcard was made in Germany, as were the majority of postcards sold in the United States before World War I.

The Key Route Pier is pictured here from the shore. The Key System was the privately-owned mass-transit system that prevailed in the San Francisco East Bay from 1903 to 1960. The Key Route Pier serviced the system, allowing passengers to cross San Francisco Bay before the San Francisco–Oakland Bay Bridge was completed in 1936. The pier extended 17,000 feet into the bay along the same path the bridge would later take where passengers would then transfer to the ferry.

On this real-photo postcard, Pier Avenue is shown branching off Highway 1, the Pacific Coast Highway (which would be visible just beyond the bottom of the photograph), and leading straight to Pier Plaza, which contained an auditorium in Hermosa Beach in Los Angeles County. This concrete pier lasted from 1914 until 1944, when it was condemned after storm damage.

Court Flight, Highest Point in Los Angeles, Cal.

The Court Flight funicular, located in what is now the Court of Historic American Flags in downtown Los Angeles, was a cable railway that ran from Broadway to Hill Street. It burned down in 1943. Much of Bunker Hill, which the funicular ascended, was lowered in height when it was redeveloped in the 1950s.

Eight

ENTERTAINMENT

This stadium provided residents of San Diego with a timestamp. Older residents knew it as San Diego Stadium, which it was from its completion in 1967 until 1981. Those who came of age in the 1980s and 1990s may recall it as Jack Murphy Stadium (named after the San Diego sportswriter), as it was known from 1981 to 1997. A younger generation knew it as Qualcomm Stadium, as it was called from 1997 to 2017. Some may even have called it SDCCU Stadium, its short-lived name from 2017 until its 2021 demolition. It was replaced by Snapdragon Stadium. During its time, the stadium was home to the National Football League's San Diego Chargers (from 1967 to 2016), Major League Baseball's San Diego Padres (from 1969 to 2003), and the San Diego State Aztecs (from 1967 to 2020).

This roller coaster on the boardwalk in Long Beach operated from 1902 until around 1915 at the Pike (also known as Queens Park), an amusement zone demolished in 1979. It was also known as the Air Ship and Bisby's Spiral Airship. The Teich production number of A-11792 dates this card to 1910.

The building on the left is the 1905 Long Beach Municipal Auditorium (demolished in 1932). In the center, the initial platform of the Pleasure Pier is protected from motor traffic by bollards. At the end of the pier that juts into the Pacific Ocean is the Sun Pavilion with its twin towers, which were swept away by strong waves in 1934.

PACIFIC OCEAN PARK,
Santa Monica, California

This amusement park was between Pier Avenue in the Ocean Park neighborhood and Navy Street in Venice. Located on the border of Santa Monica and Venice, it opened in 1958 and closed in 1967, with its final demolition occurring in 1974 and 1975. The Ocean Sky Ride (shown below) was an aerial tram that is also visible in the above image on the left side of the pier.

V. 29. Dance Pavilion on the Pier, Venice, California.

PIER BY NIGHT, VENICE, CAL.

The three-story building shown above was part of the Abbot Kinney Pier in Venice before it was annexed by Los Angeles in 1925. It was constructed in 1921 after a fire destroyed the old pier in 1920. The Venice Dance Hall was designed by Lawrence Furniss to allow for 1,600 people (800 couples). The pier was demolished in 1946, and any remaining structures were destroyed by a 1947 fire. The Teich production number of A-91664 dates the above card to 1922. In the image at left, the Ferris wheel on the right and the Ship Cafe behind it (toward the left) are lit up as crowds walk the midway in Venice. These structures were on the Abbot Kinney Pier. The card dates to sometime between the building of the Ferris wheel (1911) and the destruction of the pier by fire in 1920.

On the Midway, Venice, Cal.

The Midway was on the south bank of the Venice Lagoon in the period before Venice was annexed by Los Angeles in 1925. It and the lagoon were built by Abbot Kinney along with the "Venice of America" canals, a pier, and other developments on Kinney's piece of what was originally Santa Monica. The Midway was torn down in 1911 and replaced with the roller coaster called Race thru the Clouds. This undivided-back postcard was produced prior to April 1, 1907.

This building, which featured two stories with towers and an entrance with a round arch, was constructed in 1909 on the Abbot Kinney Pier in Venice. By 1910, it was the Marine Biological Station–Venice for the University of Southern California (USC), also known as the Venice Aquarium and Biological Station (in 1916). It was established as a station by Albert B. Ulrey, USC's first marine biologist. It not only provided research resources but offered summer courses for the university's students. It was destroyed when the pier caught fire in December 1920.

The Aquarium, Venice, Cal.

ENTRANCE TO IDORA PARK, OAKLAND, CAL.

Idora Park was an amusement park in the North Oakland neighborhood from 1903 to 1929. It had roller coasters, a zoo, and a skating rink. Pictured above is the front entrance to the park, which was located along the streetcar lines that ran through Oakland at the time. The below image shows a covered well at the center of the park.

Rebecca Well, "Idora Park Beautiful", Oakland, Cal.

SCENIC RAILWAY BUILDING, IDORA PARK, OAKLAND, CAL.

Idora Park depended on streetcar traffic, including many visitors who came across from San Francisco for the day. The advent of the automobile hastened the decline of the park, and no evidence of it remains today. The area covered by the park is now a residential neighborhood. Above is the scenic railway building, and below is the heart of the park.

Idora Park Beautiful, Oakland, Cal.   0518

4729. Main Entrance of
Wonderland Park,
Ocean Beach,
San Diego, Cal.

Wonderland Park, in the Ocean Beach neighborhood, was the first amusement park in San Diego. It featured the Blue Streak Racer, which was once the largest roller coaster on the West Coast. It was very popular for its first two years (1913–1914), but the opening of the Panama-California International Exhibition in Balboa Park lowered attendance to the point that Wonderland Park closed and was sold in March 1915. Storm tides in 1916 undermined the roller coaster, which was sold to an amusement park in Santa Monica, and the park was dismantled.

1023 The Chutes, Fillmore and Turk Sts., San Francisco, California

The Chutes at Fillmore was an amusement park in San Francisco with a ride, vaudeville theater, and restaurant. It covered the block bounded by Fillmore, Turk, Webster, and Eddy Streets in the heart of the Fillmore District. It opened on July 14, 1909, and burned down on May 29, 1911.

Bathhouses grew in popularity in the United States in the late 19th century as public amenities (for those who did not have running water) and for entertainment (swimming). The Los Banos bathhouse was at the foot of D Street in downtown San Diego across the street from the Santa Fe Depot. It was torn down in 1928.

This building, which housed a swimming pool, featured turrets and battlements, as shown on the postcard. It was constructed in 1925 on the southwest corner of City Park in Corona (in the Inland Empire), facing East Sixth Street, by local builder G.C. Berner. It was destroyed in 1965 to make way for a new city pool.

The Commonwealth Building was in downtown San Diego at the corner of Fifth Avenue and B Street—not to be confused with the current Commonwealth Building in downtown San Diego at the corner of First Avenue and A Street. The Pantages Theater on the corner opened in 1924 and became the RKO Orpheum in 1929. It had over 2,000 seats, though these were reduced to 1,400 by 1941. The building was demolished in 1964.

The Hollywood Theater stood at 314 F Street in downtown San Diego in the location that is now home to the Metropolitan Correction Center. The burlesque shows at the theater thrived on the sailor market before and during World War II. The burlesque industry declined heavily in the mid-1950s, and the theater closed in 1970. This picture was taken on April 10, 1943, but the original image also listed "Say No More Joe" with "The Hughes Trio" on the sign below "Big Girl Revue." More information on the theater can be found in "San Diego's Bygone Burlesque: The Famous Hollywood Theatre," by Jaye Furlonger, in the *Journal of San Diego History*.

The "new pleasure pier" was built in 1916 south of Wharf No. 1 in Redondo Beach, one of the beach cities in Los Angeles County, and lasted until 1928, although it was damaged by a storm in 1919. It has also been called the "endless" pier because it made a rough circle and returned to the beach. It was built in place of Wharf No. 2, which was demolished the same year the pleasure pier was constructed. The pier rebuilt after a fire in 1988 is made of reinforced concrete.

Fraser's Million Dollar Pier lasted less than 15 months. Built in Ocean Beach (now a neighborhood of Santa Monica in Los Angeles County, but then a separate city), it was 300 feet wide and extended 1,000 feet into the ocean, making it the largest amusement pier in the world. It opened on June 17, 1911, but was consumed by a fire that wiped out not only the park but also much of the neighborhood in just a few hours on September 3, 1912.

CAFE OF WORLD   HOUSE OF HOSPITALITY

AVENUE OF PALACES, SAN DIEGO EXPOSITION

The Panama-California International Exposition of 1915 provided San Diego's Balboa Park with a completely new look, but most of the buildings constructed for it were not intended to be permanent. The Cafe of the World, located on the northeast corner of the Plaza (upper right), existed in Balboa Park from 1915 to 1962.

The Foreign Arts Building was designed by Carleton M. Winslow (1876–1946) and built for the Panama-California International Exposition of 1915 in Balboa Park. Also known as the Foreign Liberal Arts Building, it was renamed the House of Hospitality for the California Pacific International Exposition of 1935 and subsequently demolished and rebuilt (with the 1935 name and appearance) in 1997; it is one of many buildings that appear, on first glance, to have survived but are actually replicas of the originals.

The Home Economy Building is pictured here during the Panama-California International Exposition of 1915. This was also known as the Pan-Pacific Building, the Cafe of the World, and the American Legion Building.

This is a real-photo postcard of the Southern California Counties Building during the Panama-California International Exposition of 1915, held in San Diego's Balboa Park to celebrate the completion of the Panama Canal. This building burned down in 1925 only hours before it was to host the annual fireman's ball. It was located where the San Diego Natural History Museum now stands.

The Japanese Tea Pavilion (or Tea House or Tea Garden), located northeast of the Botanical Building, was built by the Japanese Tea Association and the Japanese and Formosan governments for the Panama-California International Exposition of 1915. Maintained by the Asakawa family until 1941, it was then used by the US military during World War II and finally razed in 1955. The area where it stood is now the Children's Zoo feature of the San Diego Zoo.

Residents of San Diego would be surprised to find two of the city's most iconic landmarks, the California Tower and the Cabrillo Bridge—both built for the Panama-California International Exposition—in a book of lost places. It is the lagoon in the heart of Balboa Park, however, that is lost. It was not natural but was also constructed for the exposition. The lagoon was filled in when the construction of State Route 163 was completed through the canyon in the park in 1948.

These postcards offer two different views of the Palace of Photography, which was built for the Panama-California International Exposition of 1915 as the Science and Education Building and subsequently known as the Medical Arts Building and the Veterans of Foreign Wars Building (also called the War Memorial Building). It was razed in the 1960s.

AMERICA'S EXPOSITION, SAN DIEGO, CALIFORNIA   SA-H1146

The Firestone Singing Fountain was first displayed at the California Pacific International Exposition of 1935 in Balboa Park in San Diego. Standard Oil's Tower of the Sun is in the distance, with the fountains in the foreground. The changing colors of the water were controlled by music. The fountains were paved over in 1936, after the completion of the exposition, and the site was converted into a parking lot.

Palm Canyon Bridge was a wooden footbridge constructed for the California Pacific International Exposition of 1935 so that guests could view the palm trees planted for the Panama-California International Exposition of 1915. It also provided a shortcut from the Alcazar Gardens parking lot to a spot across the street from the Spreckels Organ Pavilion in San Diego's Balboa Park. The bridge was torn down in the 1950s.

TOWERS OF PALACE OF FOODS AND BEVERAGES,

The Towers of Palace of Foods and Beverages was later reconstructed as the Casa del Prado. It was constructed for the Panama-California International Exposition of 1915 as the Agricultural and Horticultural Building; it later became the Varied Industries & Food Products Building, then was renamed the Foreign and Domestic Products Building (known for many years as the Food and Beverages Building) in 1916. It was briefly known as the San Diego County Fair Building before being demolished in 1969, with the Casa del Prado opening in 1971.

Nine

HOUSES

Imperial Beach, Cal.

Residence of U.S. Grant, San Diego, Cal.

Dear:— I do miss you so wish you could spend a week end with me at the Beach. Will write soon! lots of love . . .

This undivided-back postcard shows the home of Ulysses S. Grant Jr., the son of the 18th president of the United States. The Havermale Mansion at the corner of Eighth and Ash Streets was purchased by the Grants in 1893. The house, built in 1887–1888 by Ora Hubbell, was designed by the same architects who created the Hotel del Coronado—James W. and Merritt Reid. It was demolished in 1927 to make way, ironically, not for the U.S. Grant Hotel, which Grant Jr. built himself, but for the El Cortez Hotel. Undivided-back postcards often had blank spaces around the edges that could be filled in by messages to the recipient, such as those shown on this card.

EDWARDS POST CARDS, L. A.   Anna Held's Ark, La Jolla, California

Anna Held was a former governess for Ulysses S. Grant Jr. In 1894, she bought much of the hillside above La Jolla Cove in what was then a mostly undeveloped area north of San Diego (it is now a neighborhood of San Diego). She founded the Green Dragon Colony, building 12 houses in all, each of them distinctive. The Ark (above) was a boat-shaped structure complete with portholes and a prow facing the Pacific Ocean. Below, the Ark is visible at far left. Held sold the colony in 1912 for $30,000, and over the years, almost all of the houses were torn down. What remains can be glimpsed between Prospect Street and Coast Boulevard on the hillside above the cove.

Anna Held's Ark and Vicinity, La Jolla, Cal.

Dr. A.G. Castles' Mansion Sans Souci
Hollywood, Cal.

Castle Sans Souci ("castle without a care") was built in 1912 by Dr. Alfred Castles (born Schloesser, meaning "castles"), who changed his name during World War I to avoid anti-German sentiment in the United States. This was his second castle, the first having proved to be too small. The castle was torn down in 1928, and the Castle Argyle Apartments sit in its place just above the Hollywood Freeway at the base of the Hollywood Hills. Not all postcards were designed to be an image-based reminder of a trip to send to friends and relatives. Postcards were heavily used in advertising, as shown here, as there is nowhere on the card to include an address, in spite of it having a place for a stamp. This postcard dates to between 1918 and 1928.

The mansion on the 56-acre estate purchased by Douglas Fairbanks in 1919 for his bride, Mary Pickford, is pictured here from the gates of the drive. It was designed by architect Wallace Neff (1895–1982). The mansion's name, Pickfair, was coined by newspaper staff from the combined last names of these two famous film stars who would later divorce. The house was demolished around 1990. The Teich production number of 88456 dates the card to 1922.

The Robert and Clara Burdette home was constructed in the South Arroyo neighborhood of Pasadena in Los Angeles County for Clara Baker Burdette and her first husband, Robert, in 1892. It was also known as Sunnyside or Sunnycrest. It was demolished in 1926.

Hueter Residence
Santa Barbara, Cal.

This home, called El Mirasol, filled a city block in Santa Barbara. It was designed in 1905 by New York architects Delano and Aldrich for Mary Herter (whose name is misspelled on this card). In 1913, shortly after this card was produced, her heirs turned the home into the El Mirasol Hotel. In 1966, fire damage threw the property ownership into a state of continual flux that ended with the buildings being razed and donated to the City of Santa Barbara in 1975. The site was eventually used for the Alice Keck Park Memorial Gardens. The Teich production number of A-13909 dates the card to 1911.

A Garden Scene in California.
Durand Residence,
Pasadena.

A 50-room, three-story reconstruction of a French Norman chateau stands in the distance at far right behind a garden with trees and flowers. The Durand home on Millionaire's Row in Pasadena had Cherokee roses planted along Arlington Drive, which is at right in this image. The home was designed by F.L. Roehrig, completed in 1905, and razed in 1961. The site is now the Arlington Garden. This is an example of an early divided-back postcard from 1907; the back is divided but still does not allow for a message, thus the empty space on the bottom of the front of the card.

Millionaire mine owner Alva D. Myers's home on Ocean Avenue was once the most expensive residence in Long Beach. The above postcard features a view from the street, while the below image shows the view from the beach. The house was destroyed in the 1933 Long Beach earthquake.

Oakland, Cal. F. M. Smith's Ideal Home.

Frances Marion "Borax" Smith made a fortune in borax mining and would later own the Key System that provided mass transit to Oakland. He built Oak Hall mansion (the front is shown above, and the pond in the back is shown below) on the large estate he owned, Arbor Villa. After Smith's death in 1931, the estate was broken up, and the mansion was demolished. Today, over 100 houses stand on the portion of the Ivy Hill neighborhood of Oakland that was once occupied by Arbor Villa.

The Hollywood home of painter Paul de Longpré (1855–1911) was built in 1901 and designed by architect Louis Bourgeois. After an 1896 New York exhibit brought him fame, de Longpré, known for his paintings of flowers like those in the gardens shown above, moved to Hollywood in 1899. The interior of the home is pictured below. The house was demolished around 1920.

Shown above is the back of the house of Paul de Longpré. His home and garden constituted a stop on the Balloon Excursion run by the Los Angeles streetcar companies. The painter himself is pictured below inside the house among some of his artwork.

This was the Japanese tea garden at the John D. Spreckels house in Coronado, California. Spreckels, who developed much of Coronado, lived in a mansion that would later become the Glorietta Bay Inn across the street from the Hotel del Coronado. The tea garden existed at the mansion from 1908 to 1939.

This was one of multiple houses owned by renowned opera star Ernestine Schumann-Heink in the San Diego area; one of the houses still stands on Mount Helix. This Coronado house was built in 1907 by John D. Spreckels, who owned much of Coronado, for his attorney, Harry L. Titus. The house was sold to Schumann-Heink in 1923, and she lived there until just before her death in 1936. The house was demolished in 1948 and is now the location of Union Bank. The Teich production number of 106124 dates the card to 1925.

Ten

ODDS AND ENDS

This real-photo postcard shows the gateway and wall of China City in Los Angeles. When the original Chinatown in Los Angeles was razed in the 1930s to build Union Station, two competing replacements arose a few blocks away. China City was the idea of Christine Sterling, who had headed the revitalization of Olvera Street; it was completed in 1938 and made use of sets from the 1937 film *The Good Earth*. It was a walled one-block enclave bordered by Spring, Old, Main, and Macy (now Cesar Chavez) Streets. It burned down in 1948, and the remnants were razed in 1955.

Light House, Golden Gate, San Francisco, California

Mile Rocks Lighthouse was in the Pacific Ocean off the coast near San Francisco. It was built in reaction to a 1901 shipwreck and opened in 1906. In 1966, the lighthouse was replaced by a helipad.

Thousands of pigeons roost along buildings at the pigeon farm. The pigeon farm was a large breeding farm used to raise pigeons for meat at the confluence of the Los Angeles River and the Arroyo Seco. It was established in 1892 and destroyed in a flood on February 21, 1914. This undivided-back postcard was produced sometime before March 31, 1907.

A real-photo postcard of the Campfire Amphitheater in Big Basin Redwoods State Park shows how it blended into its natural environment. Big Basin Redwoods State Park, founded in 1902, is California's oldest state park and contains numerous redwood trees exceeding 250 feet in height. The amphitheater was destroyed in the CZU Lightning Complex fires in August 2020, which devastated much of the park.

No. 547
Tower of Legends
Forest Lawn Memorial-Park, Glendale, Calif.

The Tower of Legends was built in 1924 in Forest Lawn Memorial Park in Glendale, a suburb of Los Angeles, to disguise a water tower. It was torn down on April 2, 1948. Notable celebrities buried at Forest Lawn during the period that the Tower of Legends stood include Lon Chaney, Douglas Fairbanks, W.C. Fields, Jean Harlow, Carole Lombard, Will Rogers, and Irving Thalberg.

The National Orange Show Building in San Bernardino opened in 1925 to house the exposition. Although that structure burned down in 1949, subsequent buildings were erected on the same property. The 1932 exposition (pictured) commemorated the 200th anniversary of the birth of George Washington with (as described on the back of the card) "patriotic decorations blending with decorations of the Olympic Games," which were being held that summer in nearby Los Angeles.

The Blythe Sports Arena (misspelled as Blyth on the back of the card) was in Olympic Valley in Placer County in Northern California. The arena was built in 1959 and opened in 1960 to host the 1960 Winter Olympics. It was demolished in 1983.

The second USS *California* (ACR-6) was launched on April 28, 1904, and commissioned on August 1, 1907, at the Mare Island Shipyard northeast of Vallejo, California. The shipyard closed in 1996, and the *California*, after being renamed the *San Diego* in 1914, was sunk off Fire Island, New York, on July 19, 1918. The wreck is listed in the National Register of Historic Places and is a popular destination for scuba diving.

Sunset Cliffs lie alongside the Pacific Ocean side of Point Loma in San Diego. At the time of the Panama-California International Exposition in 1915, Albert Spalding, retired Hall of Fame baseball player and part owner of the Chicago White Sox, who lived in Point Loma near what was then the Theosophical Institute, spent $2 million to construct bridges, trails, benches, and a stairway in what he called Sunset Cliffs Park. The city eventually acquired the land; much of the park was eroded, so the city removed the rest due to safety concerns.

1169 Stone Steps to the Parapet, Sutro Heights, San Francisco

Adolph Sutro owned Cliff House and the Sutro Baths in northwest San Francisco. At his mansion, located across Point Lobos Avenue from Cliff House and the baths, he filled the grounds with statues and built-up battlements. The battlements still stand in what is now Sutro Heights Park, but the statues were removed when the mansion was torn down in 1939.

Entrance to the Selig Zoo,
Eastlake Park, Los Angeles, Cal.

This is the entrance to the Selig Zoo, which was located across the street from Eastside Park (now Lincoln Park) in the Lincoln Heights neighborhood of Los Angeles. Selig Zoo was owned by silent-film mogul William Selig and opened in 1913, and while it succeeded for a time in renting animals for motion pictures (including several Tarzan films), it never turned into the full-scale amusement park Selig envisioned and was sold when Selig's fortunes dwindled during the Great Depression. It is now the site of Pueblo de Los Angeles High School. The Teich production number of A-61998 dates the card to 1915.

New Band Stand and Surf, Long Beach, Cal.

The Band Stand and Surf in Long Beach stood at the end of the beach near where the Pine Avenue Pleasure Pier began. It was demolished in 1975.

Owen's Electric Tower, located at the corner of Santa Clara and Market Streets in downtown San Jose, made for a unique sight in the daytime and also when it was lit up at night. Standing 207 feet tall, it was constructed in 1881 and destroyed by a storm in December 1915. The tower lit up the downtown area with arc lights. A half-size replica was later placed at History Park, located in Kelley Park in San Jose.

INDEX

ABOUT THE JOHN AND JANE ADAMS POSTCARD COLLECTION

The John and Jane Adams Postcard Collection documents over 100 years of history and communication. The collection includes almost 1,000 postcards of San Diego County, over 4,000 from California, and over 200,000 cards from all over the world. The current scanned collection is just a fraction of the total collection that will continue to grow in San Diego State University's Digital Collections. It can be found online at digitalcollections.sdsu.edu/adamspostcards.

John Adams joined the faculty of San Diego State Teachers College in 1928 and stayed with the school through several changes of its name. After his retirement as chairman of humanities in 1968, Adams became a part-time university archivist for what was then San Diego State College. John and his wife, Jane, donated generously to the university. Their donations consisted of books, postcards, ephemera, and manuscripts. In 1989, the postcards were delivered to the Special Collections & University Archives of San Diego State University, which John had helped found. All of the postcards featured in this book are part of this collection.

The Department of Special Collections & University Archives (SCUA) houses rare, fine, unique, and valuable books, periodicals, manuscripts, and documents that require preservation, security, and care in handling. Other valuable historical items such as photographs, prints, postcards, memorabilia, scrapbooks, and oral histories are also held in Special Collections. University Archives holds material that documents the history of San Diego State University since its founding as a Normal School in 1897. The John and Jane Adams Postcard Collection is housed in SCUA.

The Digital Collections unit of the San Diego State University Library not only digitizes archival and historical materials from the Special Collections & University Archives but has active partnerships with other university, community, and international organizations to increase access to archival materials. The unit's work is available at digitalcollections.sdsu.edu.

DISCOVER THOUSANDS OF LOCAL HISTORY BOOKS FEATURING MILLIONS OF VINTAGE IMAGES

Arcadia Publishing, the leading local history publisher in the United States, is committed to making history accessible and meaningful through publishing books that celebrate and preserve the heritage of America's people and places.

Find more books like this at
www.arcadiapublishing.com

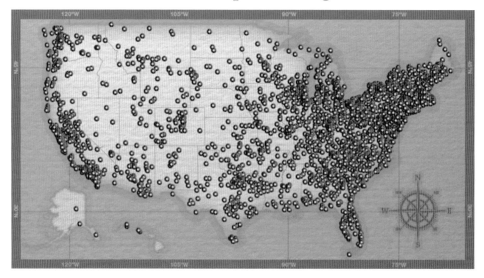

Search for your hometown history, your old stomping grounds, and even your favorite sports team.

Consistent with our mission to preserve history on a local level, this book was printed in South Carolina on American-made paper and manufactured entirely in the United States. Products carrying the accredited Forest Stewardship Council (FSC) label are printed on 100 percent FSC-certified paper.

MADE IN THE USA